THE INTERN SPEAKS MANY LANGUAGES

ELISSE M. GABRIEL
SANDRA WARD

classroom
CONNECT

Acknowledgments

Senior Product Developer—Sandra Ward
Writer—Elisse M. Gabriel
Editor—Lynn Clark
Creative Director—Heidi Lewis
Interior Designers—Megan White, Tammy Tribble
Cover Design—Amparo del Rio
Art Buyer—Jane Leibowitz
Production—Christy McDonald
Manufacturing—Benjamin Cintas

Photographs courtesy of Pei Cobb Freed & Partners.

Due to the changing nature of the Internet, site addresses and their content may vary.

Corporate Office
2221 Rosecrans Boulevard, Suite 221
El Segundo, CA 90245

Product Development Office
1241 East Hillsdale Boulevard
Foster City, CA 94404

http://www.classroom.com

ISBN: 0-932577-78-4
Printed in the United States of America
1 2 3 4 5 6 7 8 9 10 · 02 01 00 99 98

The Power of Stories   2

About This Book   4

Language and the Internet   6

FAN FANG'S STORY
An Online Chinese Newsletter   8
An Interview with Fan Fang   11
Gallery   16
Setting up an Online Newsletter   18

SHARON DUMAS' STORY
Spanish is Spoken Here   22
An Interview with Sharon Dumas   25
Gallery   30
Connecting Students with Native Language Speakers   32

GARY ANKNEY'S STORY
International Exchange Through the Internet   36
An Interview with Gary Ankney   39
Gallery   44
Connecting with the World   46

Your Story: Building a Project of Your Own   50

Resources   58

TABLE OF CONTENTS

Why stories?

Who doesn't love a good story? Stories are an age-old and powerful way of engaging the imagination. Stories can entertain, inform, educate, inspire, even bring about reform.

We at Classroom Connect have read many inspiring stories told by teachers of how the Internet has impacted their classrooms and enhanced their curriculum. We invited several teachers to share their experiences in this series of books titled *Cyberstories*. Many of the stories appearing in this series were solicited through requests we sent out on mailing lists and Usenet groups for K–12 teachers, where teachers often share stories with one another.

One fascinating aspect of the community the Internet has fostered has been the eagerness of educators to share information, advice, ideas, and stories with one another. It is our hope that these stories will serve as a foundation on which other teachers will build.

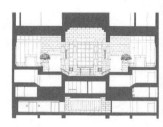

Who are the storytellers?

The storytellers in this book are "ordinary" educators who have provided their students with "extraordinary" experiences because of their willingness to step out and try new things. They are people who know the reality of the daily demands of teaching and of finding the time to keep up with technological advances. Some of the stories come from elementary school teachers of self-contained classrooms, while others come from middle and high school teachers in various subject areas, computer training coordinators, or library/media specialists.

The tales told in the *Cyberstories* series give you a glimpse into classrooms with students from a range of socioeconomic and cultural backgrounds and situations where the availability of technology varies greatly. These stories celebrate the ingenuity, curiosity, creativity, thirst for knowledge, drive to communicate, and sheer joy in learning that exists in American schools today.

THE POWER OF STORIES

Who are these stories for?

The stories presented in the *Cyberstories* series are relayed by teachers from grades one through twelve and have been supplemented with project guidelines and ideas intended for use by elementary, middle school, and high school teachers.

Just because a story has taken place in the classroom of a primary level teacher or has been conveyed by a computer training coordinator does not mean that the project must be limited to use only at that grade level or in the context of that particular subject matter. Very often, project ideas that have been successful at one grade level or in one particular subject context can be undertaken with success at many other levels and in many other contexts as well. The scope, focus, and sophistication of the same basic project idea may vary from grade to grade and even from class to class, depending on how the teacher and students shape the project and make it their own.

In fact, we have found the use of technology to be very adaptable and a great equalizer. Students in grades one through twelve, for example, have participated in projects that involve email or exchanges with Web sites. The information exchange sometimes involves connections between students of different grade levels or between students and adults.

How can stories make a difference?

It's what the reader chooses to do in response to the story that makes all the difference. We hope that you will take away from each story not only the ideas about what can be done with technology in your classroom, but also the encouragement that it can be done and the vision to recognize the impact of even the simplest Internet projects on students of all ages.

Like all good stories, these are meant to be shared—with colleagues, students, parents, community leaders—anyone who has an interest in today's students and the future of education. It is our hope that through reading stories about the ways the Internet is used in schools, you will become inspired to explore the ever-evolving world of educational technology and gain experiences worth sharing with others.

CONCEPT
As with an architectural project, preceding the design and execution of a project of any type, there is a beginning, an initial source of inspiration. Chinese-born American architect I.M.Pei did much of the conceptual work in his mind, and started with very simple sketches, to which details were added in consultation with his design team. Out of this teamwork there evolved a design "language" that reflected the architectural firm.

What are the stories in this book about?

The stories in this book all relate to the theme of students in American schools connecting with non-English speakers locally and internationally through the Internet. Each story, however, differs in terms of the languages spoken, the cultures encountered, and the modes of online technology used to communicate.

The first story focuses on the creation of an online Chinese newsletter written by Chinese-American ESL students and aimed at peers in the U.S. and Asia. The second describes the ways in which Hawaiian students are learning Spanish through online interaction with native Spanish speakers in Latin America, Mexico, and Europe. The third story recounts the progressively creative ways in which foreign exchange students communicated with friends and family back home using audio and visual online technology. Common among these projects are teachers and students who were willing to explore new technologies and learn through experience, all of whom succeeded in traveling the Internet using the latest in multilingual technology.

How can the stories in his book be used to create Internet projects?

Following the summary of each story, there is an interview with the storyteller that provides additional information and background material explaining how the Internet project was conducted and organized. For each story, we have also devoted two Gallery pages featuring student work and writing that allows you to view the story from a different perspective. Finally, for each story we present guidelines you can use to create a similar project of your own.

After the presentation of all three stories, we conclude with a section titled "Your Story." Here we offer guidelines for working with students to brainstorm ways they can communicate to non-English speakers via the Internet, and suggest resources that might facilitate potential projects.

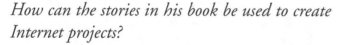

ABOUT THIS BOOK

What is the relationship between teaching and technology in successful Internet projects?

Many teachers today are asking the question, "How can I use the Internet to teach_____?" There is great interest in exposing students to this exciting new technology, and great hope for its potential as a learning tool. One important thing to keep in mind is that the Internet is a means to an end, rather than an end in itself. It provides a window to the world in ways we never imagined, but must be used with a particular goal in mind in order to become truly effective as a teaching and learning medium.

FUNCTION
An important consideration in Pei's work was the way in which the building would be used. Function was considered before form, with the ideal goal being the integration of form and function.

Educators need to view the Internet as a tool for something far more significant than the technical skills required to use it—namely, the goal of educating students to become lifelong learners who will be not only valuable members of the work force of the future, but also active, contributing members of their communities—to successfully integrate this powerful medium into the curriculum. The critical thinking, research, and communication skills learned by students in projects such as those described in this and other *Cyberstories* books are essential for the future and will not become obsolete. For those who have harnessed the power of the Internet in their own classroom projects, the question eventually becomes, "How could I have taught this without the availability of the Internet?"

What skills and equipment do teachers need to conduct projects like these?

There is a tremendous range in the sophistication and cost of the equipment described in each story. All began with existing school equipment, which ranged from the simple use of email and wordprocessors to state-of-the-art language translation programs and language digitizers. One teacher acquired additional hardware and software through grant applications and community donations.

Likewise, the technical training of the teachers varies. One of the three teachers in this book works as a computer instructor and began with a degree of technical knowledge that increased as he encountered new technologies throughout the school year. Another is a foreign language teacher who took teacher workshops to learn more about MOO and Muddweller technology. The third, an ESL resource instructor, learned about technology through his role as a software evaluator, in addition to taking related courses in U.S. colleges and in China.

"Internetional" communication

The advent of Web technology makes it possible for us to "visit" other countries without so much as stepping foot outside the classroom. It's an invaluable aid in the process of learning languages as it promotes international communication with peers who are eager to exchange information, share ideas, and teach one another. In this way, the Internet surmounts the borders not only between countries, but also continents, allowing firsthand interchange through the World Wide Web.

Culturally speaking

Part of learning a language is understanding its associated culture. Futurist and visionary, David Thornburg, writes, "While advances in translation technology are occurring daily, the process of learning a new language also exposes the learner to the culture in which that language is used. This cultural component is essential for effectively conducting business on a world-wide basis." (2020 Visions for the Future of Education, http://www.tcpd.org/handouts/thornburg/2020visions.html, April 15, 1997) Understanding a country's culture—the religion on which it is based, the history behind it, its customs, morés—lends meaning to the way their language is used and creates a foundation of mutual understanding.

Whether your goal is to have students practice a foreign language, learn about other cultures, or communicate with people around the world, the Internet can serve as an invaluable teaching aid, exposing students to language and culture firsthand, thereby increasing their awareness, tolerance, and curiosity about people beyond the English-speaking mainland of the United States.

Now read the stories. Share them with your colleagues and your students. Let the inspiration of these stories guide your beginning steps toward connecting your school with the world. Watch your own story grow.

FOUNDATION

"If you have built castles in the air, your work need not be lost; that is where they should be. Now put foundations under them."

—Henry David Thoreau

An Online Chinese Newsletter

A native of the People's Republic of China, Fan Fang immigrated to the USA in 1987. He currently works as the EIA/LEP program director and ESL/Bilingual department head at Abraham Lincoln High School in San Francisco.

Having come to the states less than a decade ago, Fan recognized the difficulty in adapting to a new country and entirely different school system. Many of his Chinese immigrant students had limited English proficiency, did not understand their textbooks, class schedules, or even how to dress for gym class. Some students were mistakenly placed in lower-level classes because they were thought to be slow rather than limited in English language skills.

Luckily, these students were able to turn to Fan, who began introducing key English literacy concepts through the use of translation software on the Internet. As a bilingual teacher, he was well aware that his students would actually learn English better by establishing solid literary skills in their first language of Chinese, then transferring these skills back to English.

With the aid of a $1000 grant from the San Francisco Education Fund, Fan began his project by teaching students how to communicate on the Internet via email, with the initial goal of providing students with the opportunity to practice writing in Chinese. As students established more global connections, Fan found it difficult to monitor the educational value of this correspondence, and decided that an online publication would be a logical next step. Through a newsletter publication, students

FAN FANG'S STORY

could practice the use of Chinese in a meaningful context while learning important skills such as creative writing, editing, graphic design, research, data-analysis, and interviewing. The students' email pals could then contribute to the newsletter, making it a cooperative, educational project.

In less than one school year, the students completed 20 newsletters! Fan acted as the main advisor, but let students take creative reign of the publication. Students formed an editorial board and brainstormed to generate ideas.

In each issue, the students decided there would be five set columns: school news, campus chat, features, sports corner, and people, as well as a focus question for students to write about. The "hot" topics included: Should public schools prohibit female students from wearing tank tops and mini-skirts to school? Should girls join the army? Are there ghosts? If you could make yourself into an ideal person, what would you be like? Contributors included not only local middle and high school students, but also those from China, Taiwan, and the United Kingdom.

Although the newsletter was created with native Chinese students in mind, there were also non-Chinese speakers who participated in the project. Some, in fact, were students who do not speak the Chinese language at all. These people worked as reporters to survey poll results or write in English about ongoings at other schools. Other non-Chinese students were participants in the school's Chinese immersion program and already knew a significant amount of Chinese. This project gave them the opportunity to practice their Chinese language skills. Both groups of students learned a great deal about the Chinese culture through their participation in this project.

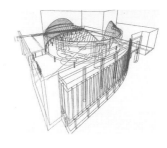

FOUNDATION
The foundation is the first step on which later efforts are based. Pei came to America to study. His training in structural engineering at MIT proved an excellent foundation for architecture, which he studied at Harvard. According to Pei, "MIT taught me…what technology stands for—what technologists and scientists are looking for is very much the same as what architects are looking for.."

Fan's newsletter has been so well-received that his school has received a new PC lab, which will enable more students to become staff writers. Next year, Fan plans to create a course called "Internet Application in Chinese," which will allow native English speakers who have been in the Chinese immersion program for over eight years the opportunity to apply their Chinese skills in real-life situations. This innovative program will be the first of its kind to be offered in the U.S., especially on a pre-college level.

To see online examples of student work, visit the student homepage at http://nisus.sfusd.k12.ca.us/programs/chinese/0897/0897m.htm. Fan Fang also invites you to come browse his Web site found at http://nisus.sfusd.k12.ca.us/programs/chinese/homepage.htm, where you will find helpful information to get you started on a similar project. Both pages are printed in English and Chinese. Read on to learn more about Fan's story in the following interview.

Q: What background did you and your students have in using technology before beginning the project?

A: When we started, my students had no background in using technology. I was mostly a computer user and had little background in the field. I learned while I was implementing the project.

Which grade levels did your project include?

We started in middle school, then we expanded it to high school level. Now it includes students in sixth to twelfth grade. In middle school, lower grade students have some difficulty getting some abstract ideas such as HTML programming in relation to Web browsers, but high school students don't seem to have this kind of confusion. It is also a more effective way to draw girls to be interested in math and science. More girls like computers than boys, even [though] sometimes they have to do some data analysis or find out how to fix a computer hardware problem. These areas are traditional "boy" areas, but girls are doing better than boys.

How did students get involved?

Students were involved through their primary language arts classes, after-class clubs, and bilingual classes.

How much class time was required to implement the newsletter project?

We had a 45-minute elective called "Internet Application in Chinese" every day for students to learn and to work on their online Chinese magazine.

What hardware did you use?

- IBM compatible computers (486/66 MHz or better; the "Headquarter server" is a Pentium 200 MHz with MMX, 64 MB of SDRAM and 4.3 GB of hard disk on a Windows NT network with ethernet connection to the district's Internet service)
- Modem (for home connection)
- HP Deskjet 4p scanner
- Penpower Chinese language digitizer
- Wisdom pen Chinese language digitizer
- Twinbridge Chinese pen Chinese language digitizer

Could you tell us more about the Chinese translation technology?

We use an online translation program called Transperfect by American Insign, Inc. It can turn an English Web page into Chinese in seconds and translate a single sentence or a whole document from English to Chinese in minutes. The accuracy rate is over 80%.

We don't use the translation program in our online magazine. It was used for helping students in their research and writing skill development. Machines will never be 100% accurate in terms of grammar and meaning. But this product does a pretty good job in conveying meanings.

Who supports all the equipment to keep it running, make changes, etcetera?

I am the techie person who takes care of my equipment in my department because our technology teacher and his two assistants—trained students—don't have that much time to take care of a big network, a couple hundred computers, and a TV broadcasting station at the same time in our 2400-student high school.

How did you acquire additional technology for the school? Language fonts and keypads?

Fonts are not enough because we need individual software for each machine. Writing pads are not always needed depending on the levels of the student. There are many ways to acquire computers and software. Writing grants, seeking business support, and getting the district and school administration to support the program are some ways that we find successful.

How did your use of technology change throughout the school year?

At the first stage of our project, we had only one computer so that each group had to share. While one group was working online, the other groups were writing and editing their articles. Now, because most of

"Technology is not my personal interest, but teaching is my big interest."

our participants have computers at home, they can do their writing at school and type it up in Chinese at home and email to the "headquarter server" for publishing.

How did the project work out for the students?

The students loved every piece of our project. They got to email their favorite pop singers. They knew more about their favorite cartoon characters. They found answers to their math and science problems. They got A++ in their social studies reports. But the most amazing achievement is that most of the ESL participants have been showing a more rapid mastery of the English language reflected by standardized tests such as CTBS.

What do you believe contributed most to this accelerated mastery of the English language?

Using Chinese [i.e., one's first language] to improve English comes from the theory of bilingual education. People learn to read only once in their lifetime and they learn their literary skills easily from their first language to second language. They will be doing better than those who have to struggle with a new language without any support. Computer and Internet stuff are just tools that help the students to achieve the goal of learning language through content to have more meaning and more fun.

What differences are you aware of between students in China and the United States?

There isn't much difference in middle school, but in high school, yes. We have some issues:

- the differences of the educational systems and expectations of students;
- the differences between the concept of Chinese print and English print (traditional Chinese goes from up to down, right to left, and some students tried to produce this in their email and it didn't work);
- the issue of traditional characters and simplified characters: although the computer does a fairly good job of converting different codes and kinds of character sets, students still have problems with the use of the characters in different contexts;
- western culture vs. Chinese culture. For example, students in China would not understand why American teachers teach their students how to write a cute love letter on Valentine's Day since in most parts of China, "dating" has a special meaning: You don't date a person if you don't plan to marry him/her.

What methods did you use for evaluating student achievement or objectives?

• Portfolio of students' writing

• Student Web page using an adopted rubric

• Standardized test

What future plans do you have for other projects or for expanding your online publication?

We have purchased a PC lab with a class set of computers and Chinese language digitizers. This will be the first high school computer lab in the nation that students can work on his/her Internet project in Chinese

"Computer and Internet stuff are just tools that help the students to achieve the goal of learning language"

individually. We will also start a two-way Chinese immersion program at high school level to include more immersion students to participate in our program. It will lean toward producing highly professional skills [for] Chinese computer users. Currently, a Chinese wordprocessor is very difficult to find, and companies pay big $$$ for anyone who knows Chinese HTML.

Here is a printout of the student online newsletter, in both Chinese and English. More issues can be found online at http://nisus.sfusd.k12.ca.us/programs/chinese/clflyr.htm.

The Colorful Years
浪漫年華

Volume 2 Issue 9   **May 30, 1997**

FROM THE DISTRICT
SFUSD Language Academy Celebrates First Annual Language Olympics

The newly formed SFUSD Language Academy celebrates its innovative model of language acquisition and use of high technology on Saturday, May 10, 1997, when it recognized students' bilingual abilities.

Thirty bilingual students were honored at the First Annual Language Olympics for their language acquisition and academic excellence. The contest attracted more than 500 applicants from the 4th - 12th grades. The students wrote in fifteen different languages about why it is important to know more than one language.

"SFUSD's goal is to ensure student literacy in at least two languages. The Language Olympics Program celebrates our students' academic achievements within a multicultural and multilinguistic world, " comments Dr. Waldemar Rojas, Superintendent of Schools.

Medals were awarded for the top three presentations in each language and grade category. All participants received a Certificate of Recognition. As part of the Language Olympics ceremony, the Language Academy honored its bilingual, ESL, and world language teachers in commemoration of Teachers' Day.

Dr. Rosa Apodaca, Assistant Superintendent and Director of the Language

Language Olympics: Chinese winners and the Board of Supervisors: Ms. Teng and Dr. Yu
語言奧林匹克比賽的中文獲獎者和市參事鄧式美和余鎮良（右一）

TOPIC

Academy says that, "I am delighted with the outpouring of support for SFUSD's challenging new approach to language acquisition. This program puts the District on the cutting-edge of supporting and realizing the importance of a multilingual society. "

新成立的三藩市校區語言學院於五月十號星期六在證粉華山初中舉行第一屆全市語言奧林匹克比賽頒獎大會，以表揚學生的雙語能力。

三十個雙語學生在表揚大會上被授予獎牌及獎品。教育局長、各部領導以及三藩市的市參事鄧式美，余鎮良 等出席頒獎。三藩市無線26號電視台主播斯美齡擔任主持。這次活動吸引了500多位4年級到12年級的學生參加。學生們用15種不同的語言寫了為什麼懂得多於一種

語言是很重一的。

"三藩市聯合校區的目標就是要保證學生能掌握至少兩種語言。語言奧林匹克就是在多文化和多語言的世界裡面慶祝學生的學術成就。" 教育局長羅夏時博士。

除了授與每一個語言組前三名的得獎

Inside This Issue 在這一期：

1	語言奧林匹克比賽頒獎
2	富蘭克林初中教師贏得大獎
3	白雁卡的告別辭
4	怎樣給女孩子打電話？
5	（小說）沙灘上的淚

FEATURES
Looking closely at specific examples can lead to better understanding of the overall characteristics of a general approach. Glass skylights are a recurring feature in many Pei buildings. The dramatic sweep of the curved skylights of the Morton H. Meyerson Symphony Center, which Pei designed for the city of Dallas, lends sculptural drama to the exterior while illuminating the interior.

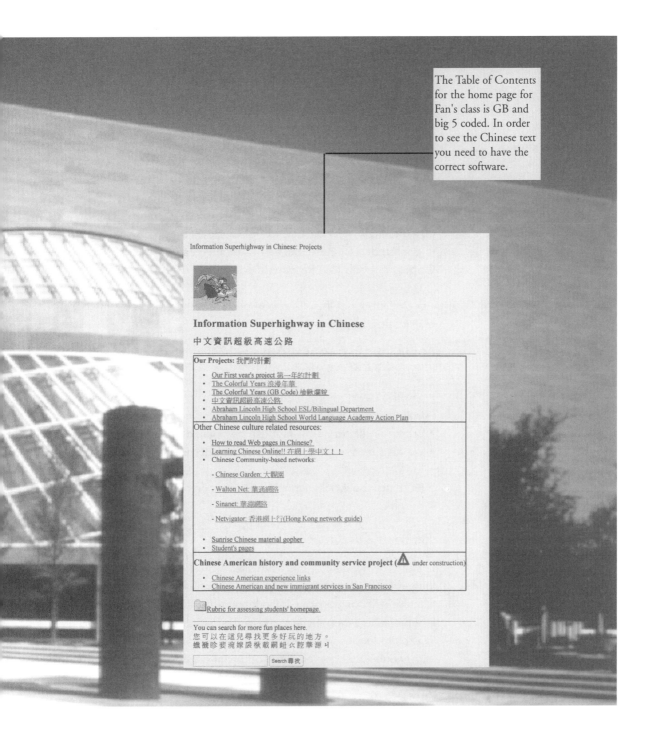

The Table of Contents for the home page for Fan's class is GB and big 5 coded. In order to see the Chinese text you need to have the correct software.

Information Superhighway in Chinese: Projects

Information Superhighway in Chinese
中文資訊超級高速公路

Our Projects: 我們的計劃
- Our First year's project 第一年的計劃
- The Colorful Years 浪漫年華
- The Colorful Years (GB Code) 繪歟爛钕
- 中文資訊超級高速公路
- Abraham Lincoln High School ESL/Bilingual Department
- Abraham Lincoln High School World Language Academy Action Plan

Other Chinese culture related resources:
- How to read Web pages in Chinese?
- Learning Chinese Online!! 在網上學中文！！
- Chinese Community-based networks:

    - Chinese Garden: 大觀園

    - Walton Net: 華通網路

    - Sinanet: 華淵網路

    - Netvigator: 香港網上行(Hong Kong network guide)

- Sunrise Chinese material gopher
- Student's pages

Chinese American history and community service project (⚠ under construction)

- Chinese American experience links
- Chinese American and new immigrant services in San Francisco

Rubric for assessing students' homepage.

You can search for more fun places here.
您可以在這兒尋找更多好玩的地方。
蠟襪诊娿涴嫁屓橪截嗣蚾朚瓄華源丩

[Search 尋找]

Are you and your students interested in creating an online newsletter written in a foreign language? This project is a wonderful way for students to communicate with fellow speakers of that language in an organized, consistent format.

Share Fan Fang's Story

Discuss the Chinese newsletter site with your students. Have students visit http://nisus.sfusd.k12.ca.us/programs/chinese/homepage.htm to explore the home site and receive helpful information to get started. Also visit http://nisus.sfusd.k12.ca.us/programs/chinese/0897/0897m.htm to view an example of a student site. Both sites are written in English and Chinese, but you need the correct software to view the Chinese symbols (see Resources, p.62).

Ask students what they liked best about these sites. Discuss the benefits of a foreign language newsletter.

As illustrated in Fan's story, some benefits of having an online foreign language newsletter can be:

- sharing news, information, and opinions with same-language peers both in the U.S. and abroad;
- practicing literary skills that can be applied to English;
- working as a team to create a consistent format and subject matter for the newsletter;
- learning about online language technology while practicing editing, graphic design, and research.

Research Available Resources

A major component of this newsletter project is the element of using language translation technology that help make both English and Chinese editions possible. If the language you want to work in requires different letters than those found in the English alphabet, you will need to explore language fonts. The Yamada Language Center at http://babel.uoregon.edu/Yamada.html provides an archive of non-English fonts. All fonts at this site can be downloaded directly from the

Web, and are legally distributable with no copyright issues outstanding. Translation software is also helpful in the process of switching from one language to the other in the process of developing research and writing skills. Depending on the level of the student, writing pads might be helpful as well.

A most effective way to explore resource options is by communicating directly online, whether through chat rooms, Web sites, mailing lists, and newsgroups, or email with fellow teachers (See Resources, p. 61). Another option is to talk to fellow teachers in your school or community who have or are planning to adapt similar technology to their classrooms. Speaking with a software specialist at a computer store is yet another way to explore options and find out more about the latest in language-related technology.

Establish Goals

Before delving into the newsletter itself, it's helpful to begin a publication project with a general direction or vision. Written into a simple sentence, this "mission statement" provides a distinct focus and direction. It clarifies who the audience is, what the subject parameters are, and why it's being written. Some basic questions to consider might include:

- What types of news will this newsletter include?
- Who will read it?
- What would I (the student) want to read in this sort of publication?
- How many pages should this newsletter be?
- What general subjects should we include each month?

As with Fan's student newsletter, it may be helpful to assign students different roles (or allow them to assign themselves) on the publication. Students can participate as part of an editorial board, as writers or reporters, graphic designers, and so forth. Subdividing students into groups not only organizes them, it also gives each student a distinct purpose and feeling of importance as part of the group. Further, it motivates students to excel in the areas which interest them most.

ELEMENTS
There are specific elements that can be identified in a particular style or approach. Pei's designs were characterized by geometric purity, high quality materials, innovations in technology, and attention to detail.

Once students have decided on their "jobs," they can discuss potential columns for the newsletter. The existence of columns is helpful in providing a consistent format in each issue that ensures that a variety of subjects will be covered. Fan's newsletter included five general columns: school news, campus chat, features, sports corner, and people. One method of deciding which columns to include is to look in a newspaper or magazine. Students can then brainstorm ideas before narrowing them down.

The frequency of newsletter issues may become increasingly important as students get used to the production process, but it might be easier to focus on thoroughness and completion before rushing into another issue. The length of each issue, the amount of time you and the students have to devote to the newsletter, the time of year, and group effort as a whole will all contribute towards determining how often a newsletter is produced.

Create Your Own Newsletter

Because you want others to read and respond to your newsletter, it is helpful to cultivate an "audience." Providing an email address will promote responses, especially when survey questions or feedback is requested. Since the newsletter will be written in another language, it immediately invites non-English readers to the site.

STRUCTURE

"Structure…proceeds from generals to particulars arriving at the blossom."

—Frank Lloyd Wright

Spanish is Spoken Here

A resident of Hawaii since 1969, Sharon Dumas is a high school Spanish teacher at Kailua High School in Kailua. In addition to speaking English and Spanish, Sharon also speaks French, a little Hawaiian, and German.

Sharon's approach to teaching Spanish has changed significantly with her decision to integrate online technology, specifically MOOs, into her curriculum. MOOs, object-oriented MUDs, are virtual, text-based worlds where users can connect simultaneously and interact with each other. These are slightly more sophisticated versions of MUDs, Multi-User Domains (which were used in the '80s to create, among other things, online adventure games such as Dungeons and Dragons). Their main emphasis is on social interaction and their ability to create "virtual communities."

Unlike email, a MOO user doesn't have to wait for a response. It's more like a live, interactive conversation that can involve one-on-one interaction or simultaneous conversations with several people from all over the world.

MOO's educational values are threefold: They enable real-time communication with people from around the world; allow users to enter virtual "rooms" where they can tour famous cities, take part in lab experiments or meet fictional characters; and inspire students to use their imaginations to create buildings, games, robots, and worlds, since everything in a MOO is considered an "object" by the computer.

Sharon first learned about MOO programs from an English teacher at a technology workshop. She immediately recognized the value of MOOs as a vehicle for learning Spanish, as it would allow students to practice conversing and writing in Spanish with native Spanish speakers from around the world.

Sharon began teaching students about MOOs using an English MOO, having them practice their Spanish skills with people who speak both English and Spanish. Once students became comfortable with this basic technology, she had students begin speaking with native Spanish speakers using Spanish MOOs.

The most frequently visited Spanish MOO among Sharon's students has been MundoHispanico, a group of speakers of Spanish, including teachers, students, and computer programmers, all of whom have worked together to create this virtual community. Regular "visitors" of this program include natives of Spain, Colombia, Costa Rica, Mexico, Ecuador, Peru, Panama, Venezuela, Chile, and Argentina, as well as Germany, Japan, the United Kingdom, Greece, and the United States.

Sharon assigned specific tasks for the students each time they went online, such as finding out about the person they were chatting with or about the culture of that person's country. Sharon believed this interaction would help students learn to converse like "real" Spanish speakers do.

This experience has proven quite motivating for Sharon's students. They now have a reason to learn Spanish, since they use it on a daily basis. Knowing that they will be communicating with native speakers, students are more inclined to learn new vocabulary and grammatical skills. They also enjoy reading publications such as the daily newspaper from Spanish-speaking countries and comparing differences in the ways world news is covered.

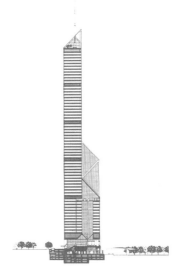

STRUCTURE
Openness to new approaches can produce surprising results. In designing the Bank of China in Hong Kong, Pei avoided the traditional, costly solution of using more steel bracing to reinforce skyscrapers against typhoon-force winds. Pei's innovative design united form and function to attain more strength with the use of less steel.

Sharon launched this project during her fourth quarter of school, a time when most teachers are winding down and completing basic requirements. Considering the time required for her to learn and practice this technology then teach it to students, this is quite a remarkable feat. Next year, Sharon plans to begin working with students on Spanish MOOs at the end of the first quarter or the beginning of the second quarter to allow students more time to explore the Internet and practice Spanish language skills.

Also in store for the future are Sharon's plans for her students to make a Web page about Hawaii in Spanish for Spanish speakers who are planning to visit. She is also working on having students produce an electronic slide show that can be published on the Web. Sharon believes that these projects, in conjunction with online language "lessons," will greatly benefit students by "demonstrating their knowledge with products rather than written tests, and teaching proficiency in a second language rather than teaching grammar and vocabulary as ends in themselves." Read the interview on the following page to find out more about Sharon's project.

Q: What background did your students have in using technology before your project began?

A: My students had been taught in first year Spanish to do email. Most of them know word processing. The concept of MOOs was new, but they caught on very quickly because we went step by step. One group learned and then taught their partners. They all seemed willing to help each other.

What curriculum areas did the project include?

This was used with Spanish II and III.

What grade levels did this project include?

My students range in grade levels from 9 to 12. This would work with any age group. I intend to try it this summer with a group of elementary students that I will be teaching. We will probably go to an English-speaking MOO.

How many students were involved?

There were about 20 students involved, about five boys, the rest girls.

What are the cultural backgrounds of these students? Any ESL, at-risk, or special needs students?

There were no ESL students, but there was one special education student. She did quite well. There was a mixture of ethnicities: Asian, Caucasian, Filipino, Puerto Rican. Classes are mixed ethnically in Hawaii.

What cultural differences did students encounter during their interaction with Spanish speakers from other countries?

Since my students were just beginning, there was not enough time to learn a lot about the culture. However, they did talk about the reversal of seasons south of the equator and about surfing spots in different parts of the world.

What hardware and software did you use for the project?

We use Mac computers and we get on to the Net with Open Transport and use Muddweller [to converse in MOOs].

Could you describe the Muddweller program?

Muddweller is a program that makes it easier to converse in a MOO because it splits the screen between the speaker and the listener—that which you read and the part where you write what you want to say. I gave my students a list of commands to practice. Most universities have installed [Muddweller]. I believe that it can be downloaded free from the Internet [http://165.248.238.26/Internet.html].

Do you have a technology coordinator on staff?

Yes, [we have someone]. He is a full-time coordinator. We also have

"My teaching has been turned upside-down in the last three years since I have had the opportunity to learn more about technology."

some alumni who help out. Ultimately, it is up to each department to take care of their own equipment.

Is there any other time allotted to teachers during the school day to do things like support the technology, get extra training, develop curriculum?

No, we are pretty much on our own. Some of us were fortunate enough to be involved in a project called Hawaii Education Research Network which was funded by the National Science Foundation. This was a three-year research project to see how technology might reform education and to set up a network of educators who could work together over the Net. We originally were in teams that developed projects and Web pages. You can check it out at: http://www.hern.hawaii.edu/hern95/pt007/.

What classroom management strategies did you use?

We went as a group to the library where the networked computers are. We took turns. The first day was to learn how to get on and speak, etc. We gradually progressed until students felt comfortable with the commands and procedures. I now have Muddweller installed on different computers around campus and the students go independently to get on the MOO.

How can other teachers learn more about MOOs? Are they useful for teaching all subjects?

I can see applications not only for teaching students, but also for collaboration among educators and administrators. It seems that it would be cheaper to talk via MOO than to travel to a central point or meet physically. I would suggest going to the Net or asking colleagues at the university level, or of course, ask the students. They [provide] a wealth of information.

What guidelines did you provide for students regarding appropriate subject matter for correspondence?

My students had each signed individual permission forms to use the Net and had done email, so they were familiar with netiquette. I gave additional explanations about MOO courtesy and reminded them not to use familiar language in Spanish. I also told them that when they were in the English MOO, that if they were gong to speak Spanish, they had to go into a room by themselves because it was not polite to speak in a language that others did not understand in front of people.

How did you monitor student exchanges?

I walked around and observed the screen to see what was being written. I also had written assignments to be completed. In the future, I will save the logs.

How do you evaluate student work?

Observation, student-written summaries in English and the target language, logs of conversations. So far, this has been mostly extra credit because everyone is still learning. Next year, I will probably require one contact a quarter second semester.

How has the Internet affected the way you teach students Spanish?

My teaching has been turned upside-down in the last three years since I have had the opportunity to learn more about technology. I use email, MOOs, Hyperstudio to make electronic slide shows, Geo Safari, computer tutorials to accompany the textbook. I feel that these are tools that assist the students in practicing real communication skills. I like to have the students use the language (vocabulary and grammar) for a

"I like to have the students use the language for a purpose rather than just learning something to cover it."

purpose rather than just learning something to cover it. The information has to connect to a real purpose or need to actually communicate something. That's why it's good to be able to communicate with native speakers, even on an elementary level.

How did the students react to learning Spanish with the aid of this new technology?

Everyone seemed willing to participate. We have to share computers and take turns because we only have a few networked computers. They first went into a room by themselves to practice before they started talking with strangers. The first day they met a surfer from South Africa. When we got on the Spanish MOO, they met people from Mexico and Columbia. It seemed to be a non-threatening way and interesting alternative to book work to practice the language.

What are your feelings about the effectiveness of the project? What were the learning benefits you saw?

Students started asking how to say things. Students have gone on their own time to converse on the MOO. I will be able to give the students the program to run at home since it is public domain software.

What do you plan to do differently next year when you start up the project again?

Next year we will start earlier in the year first with English MOOs and then with Spanish MOOs. Each time we do it, there will be specific information that the students need to gather from whomever they find at the MOOs. We will start out with easy things such as a person's name, where the person is from, and then gradually get to a point where the students talk about cultural customs, political issues, or other things of interest, perhaps a current movie, etc. At times, I will save the logs so I have a complete record of the conversations.

What advice would you offer to teachers interested in pursuing a similar project?

Colleagues and the Net are the best.

Here is the entrance to one of the MOOs visited by Sharon Dumas' students.

```
This will take you to the West Hallway.
From there, explore DaMOO.
You are here.
Obvious exits: Out (to West Hallway)
There is new activity on the following list:
*developments (#139) 125 new messages
Last connected Sat Jun 14 10:45:51

*******************ATTENTION***********************
There have been changes to the news items. Please type
"news" to get the headlines.

Elsie teleports in
adidas_guest ways, "Hi Elsie"
You ask, "Hola adidas_Guest. Cuando es tu cumpleanos?"
Happy guest says, "Hola"
Elsie says, "hi"
adidas guest says, "Remember me Sara"
Elsie says, "hola"
Elsie says "habla espanol? que bueno."
You say, "Sorry, Elsie, we are practicing in Spanish. If you
understand, join us.
```

Sharon also used a MOO to teach a course called "Fun with the World Languages." Students incorporated many languages into their conversations.

```
Tbone asks, "Teacher too?"
Elsie says, "I confess"
MOOn_Guest SMILEs
You say, "Yes these are my students, We are in a technological
collaborative classroom funded by the government. Its a wonderful
experience. I am teaching a class in world languages."
Tbone says, "Too confusing, but if I understood the language it'd
be much better than live learning."
Elsie says, "That's terrific"
loco_guest says, "Tyan le tama o leaga, e ai pisupo e ai ma leaga,
tasi lona pa e fagu fagu ai lae o KI'O uma le luga"
Pardon _Guest says, "ni hao shi wo de xingming chris"
loco_Guest en ingles por favor
I don't understand that.
Tbone nods to you and says, "I wouldn't have barged in if I
weren't invited, just so you know."
```

FEATURES

Horizontal supports in the original design of the Bank of Hong Kong broke the aluminum diagonals criss-crossing the glass skin into X's. Feng shui masters warned that this negative image, associated with the traditional calligraphy master's mark on a student's poor work, would bring bad luck. To placate the Chinese, the design was revised to give the appearance of diamonds.

High Mid Rise

High Rise

Are you and your students interested in communicating with native speakers of a foreign language? Whether your students are just beginning to learn another language or have been studying it for a number of years, the connection with native speakers provides students with the opportunity to apply what they're studying, to learn about new cultures and ways to communicate.

Share Sharon's Story

Discuss the ways in which Sharon's students communicated with native Spanish speakers using MOO technology. Have students visit and explore any number of MOO- or MUD-related sites in English to become familiar with the way these virtual environments work. Ask students to share what intrigues them most about these sites, and what they believe are the advantages of interacting with native speakers through this medium. Discuss the benefits of using online technology to learn a foreign language.

Among the benefits illustrated in Sharon's story are the following:

- learning how a language is spoken by native speakers of that language, as opposed to practiced textbook conversations
- increasing understanding about different cultures from people around the world
- feeling connected to people who speak a language besides English
- becoming motivated to learn more quickly in order to interact more effectively
- gaining the ability to "think on your feet" in a foreign language during back-and-forth online interchanges

Research Available Resources

Sharon discovered MOO technology at a teacher's workshop. There also are online "workshop" opportunities to learn about this technology. Diversity University (http://www.academic.marist.edu/duwww.htm) is one example of a Web site that provides a virtual classroom where students can work on collaborative projects using real-time communications tools.

Getting connected to a MUD or MOO is equally simple and straightforward. You simply need a personal computer, access to the Internet, and Telnet software. If you don't have Telnet, you can download a copy via ftp://ftp.classroom.net/Internet-Software/. The MOO Teacher's Tip Sheet at http://www.daedalus.com/net/MOOTIPS.html offers an overview of MOOs and how to use them in the classroom. It includes a step-by-step introduction to using a MOO and a brief history of the MOO.

There are an ever-expanding variety of educational MOOs available through the Internet. They include English, foreign language, and social MOOs. The foreign language MOOs include sites in Spanish, French, Italian, German, Portuguese, and Swedish (See Resources, pp.59-61)

Establish Goals

On a project of this nature, the main goal is not so much the completion of a product as it is learning to communicate effectively online with a person in a non-English language. An initial goal for your students may be to familiarize themselves with MOO technology.

Sharon Dumas' students were each given handouts that provide a step-by-step guide to learning about MOOs and MUDs, along with an accompanying list of commands. This page served as a helpful reference to students as they familiarized themselves with the program.

Once students are familiar with using the computer and the selected online programs, the next goal will be for students to successfully contact a native speaker of the language you're teaching. You can provide specific questions for students that will help them learn more about the person with whom they're chatting. Questions might focus around:

- the person's country, home town
- cultural/religious traditions and holidays
- family life
- education or job
- hobbies, areas of interest
- entertainment: television, movies, music

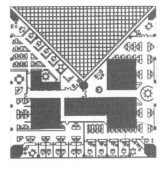

ELEMENTS
Unlike the predictability of form of traditional box-like skyscrapers, the Bank of Hong Kong has great aesthetic appeal, presenting interesting images and patterns from different vantage points.

Make the Connection

Part of making a connection online involves following certain educational guidelines and being familiar with appropriate Internet conduct. Sharon's students had each signed individual permission forms prior to using the Internet and had used email so they were familiar with "netiquette." Sharon also provided additional explanations about MOO courtesy and conversing solely in Spanish out of respect for the non-English speaker on the other end of the line. To ensure a direct connection, Sharon programmed the Muddweller so that students could click on the particular MOO and be immediately connected. This eliminated any worries about addresses.

Guidelines were provided in the handout forms, which gave specific instructions about what to ask and how to contact people. Sharon then monitored students by walking around and observing students' computer screens to see what was being written. She also required students to complete related writing assignments and keep logs of their work.

Student evaluation revolved around both teacher observation and the quality of worksheets students were required to turn in. Students were given the opportunity to earn extra-credit by further exploring the Internet's virtual MOO environments and related Spanish sites.

CRAFTSMANSHIP

"When it comes to getting things done, we need fewer architects and more bricklayers."

—*Colleen C. Barrett*

International Exchange Through the Internet

For the past 19 years, Gary Ankney has taught at Greencastle-Antrim High School in Greencastle, Pennsylvania. Originally a science teacher, Gary found new inspiration seven years ago following the completion of his master's degree in Computer Education. Since then, he has been working as the school's Computer Coordinator.

Gary's online project began as an informal means of helping foreign exchange students improve communications with home. Participants included high school and first-year college students from Germany, Russia, Thailand, and Brazil, all of whom speak some English. Although three of these students had some exposure to computers through their coursework at Greencastle-Antrim High, everyone, including Gary, was new to the Internet.

Not much planning was involved in the initial phases of this project, but rather a great deal of Internet research and exploration. "Getting the Internet in the middle of the year and teaching foreign exchange students for the first time while trying to support a school in its first year of the Teacher/Office network connection means we hit the ground running, often not knowing what was going to happen next."

The group began by using "not-so-simple email." At the time, the Internet was not yet installed on the school's computers, so students were required to write their letters on a wordprocessor and then save them onto a disk. Gary then took the disks home with him, sent the students' mail out on his computer, then brought the students their mail on the same disks.

GARY ANKNEY'S STORY

When the Internet was finally up and running at school, Gary assigned one account to all students, with all four sharing a single user ID. "This did not make for favorable international relations, with suspicions of reading one another's mail and disappearing letters occurring daily." In an effort to avert a major international incident, Gary then tried HotMail, but at the time it proved slow to download and unreliable, with several lost messages and unacceptable delays in mail postings.

Separate accounts proved to be the solution. Gary ended up giving each student an unused teacher account, provided for free by the school's Internet Service Provider (ISP). Peaceful relations were once again resumed, this time using more reliable software.

Students discovered "chat rooms" on their own. They coordinated chat sessions with friends and family, and communicated with foreign exchange students from other schools. Ying, a student from Thailand, found the language font she needed for her native language just by asking someone in a chat room.

The class's online exchanges became increasingly sophisticated as they learned how to relay messages complete with images and sound. They learned about image attachments when they wanted to look at some photographs sent to one of the students; they learned about sound when a student's brother sent an audiotape of her cat. "We sang happy birthday to Mom in Thailand (the whole class participated), and got songs (brother and friends in Germany) and pet greetings (meooowrrr!) from home. Lots and lots of pictures went back and forth." The Brazilian student showed others how he could listen to a radio station from home through the Internet, which inspired others to find ways to listen to music and news from home as well.

The school received a scanner just in time to send prom pictures home. This new technology required the class to learn about picture file formats and ways to adjust file parameters in order to get files small enough to be accepted on one family's ISP.

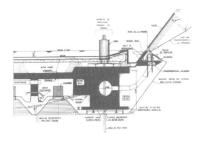

CRAFTSMANSHIP
The creation of a new entrance for the Louvre museum in Paris, and renovation of the interior of the historical building dating from 1190, was declared by Pei to be the most important project of his career. President Mitterand, who selected Pei for the project, felt that Pei's Chinese background, with its reverence for history, would combine well with Pei's American sense of innovation.

Enthusiasm reached its peak when students discovered how to communicate in their native languages online. Fonts were downloaded to be able to read the language, then keyboard drivers were installed to send out messages in that language. The Russian student put stickers on her keyboard to help with fingering (two different keyboard mappings were required to download the Cyrillic alphabet). Thai and Russian students were thrilled to be able to talk with friends and family without needing to translate words into the Latin alphabet.

Equally exciting to these students was the opportunity to share aspects of their culture with others. Two students created tours of their homeland through the World Wide Web. Another shared video clips of home and her beloved king.

Although next year will bring with it "the luxury of planning," Gary still hopes to maintain "the ability to chase down new and exciting ideas." His infectious desire to learn and explore will undoubtedly motivate students to continue searching the Internet's ever-expanding Web and discovering ways to use it to converse worldwide. Read more about Gary's story in the interview that follows.

Q: What is your role as technology coordinator?

A: I chair the district Technology Committee, which meets for a full day once a month. This year I was given a little more than a quarter of each day to pursue my technical duties, which include computer maintenance and repair, inventory, technology budgeting and purchase, student support, and teacher and staff training and support.

How much of your time is spent attending to duties related to this role during the school day? After school?

I come into school about an hour to an hour-and-a-half early each day and usually stay an hour-and-a-half or more each afternoon. Once a week I stay into the evening to get caught up and make myself available to the community. (I don't advertise it, but they find me.) I come in during the summer a day or two each week, usually for 10 hours or so. Sometimes students come in then, and I often bring my own children and their friends.

What guidelines did you provide for students involved in this international exchange project?

Work hard. Have fun. (Pretty bad, huh?) Students in courses had to keep a daily log and submit it weekly, as well as submit proposals and exit statements for all projects, and we occasionally took time for group instruction.

How did you locate international chat rooms (both English and non-English speaking) through the Internet?

Our Brazilian student (Patrick) knew all about chat and filled the others in. Marei's brother [in Germany] suggested one for her. I've helped foreign language students find appropriate chat rooms with the standard search engines (AltaVista et al.), which is how Ying (from Thailand) found hers.

Where did you obtain the various language fonts needed to communicate to other countries? How can other teachers locate such fonts and keyboard drivers?

Ying found the font she needed just by asking someone in a chat room. It was easy to download and install in Windows, but took a bit of study to figure out how to get it into Eudora and Netscape. Not too bad, really, we did figure it out by ourselves. There are people out there who would have helped us had we been stymied [See Resources p.61].

Russian was a bit harder because it can involve two completely different mappings of the keyboard. We found a lovely site [http://www.sussex.ac.uk/langc/russian.html] that explained it all, step-by-step for DOS, Windows 3.1, Windows 95 and Mac. We learned about keyboard drivers a little later, in the same way. Anastacia [our student from Russia] created a special keyboard by pasting labels on each key (we used an extra keyboard and plugged it in as needed). Ying already knew her keyboard layout.

What did incorporating audio and downloaded images entail?

Images are easy—just open them in a decent graphics package. The paint program provided in Windows doesn't read enough graphics formats to be very useful.

Using audio meant we had to learn to use the audio programs provided in Windows. They are easy to use, but we struggled a bit to figure them out. Some audio (the real-time stuff like radio) requires special drivers, but Netscape (and other browsers) will tell you what [plug-ins] you need and where to get them. It's surprisingly simple. You acquire movie drivers the same way. It only gets tough when you come across formats from different platforms (i.e. Mac to Windows, and vice versa). People on Users Groups and ListServs will get you through it [See Resources, p. 61].

What hardware/software did you use for the project?

IBM compatible computers running Windows 3.11 or Windows 95, Eudora Light, Netscape 3.0, Various plug-ins as required by individual sites, Paint Shop Pro to manipulate graphics attachments, Microtek Scanmaker E3 scanner

How did you obtain foreign language radio connections (both from the U.S. and abroad)?

Internet search engines. Only Anastacia couldn't find a radio station, but she was able to find American sites that let her listen to Russian pop and folk music.

How did access to music, full-color photos and native alphabets online affect students' approach to learning about technology?

One word: motivation. Ying turned into a real computer fanatic. She wants to buy her own computer as soon as she can save enough.

"It's a wonderful feeling when you start out with computerphobes and end up with budding experts."

She complained that it will really cut into her clothing plans. At home she hadn't liked computers, though her family has several. [She said,] "I thought the only fun thing you could do with a computer was play Solitaire."

How did you balance between teaching students and giving them free rein on this new technology?

I didn't do this well at all. I provided much too meager guidance, which confused and frustrated students at first. Once they got going, though, that wasn't such a problem. Students wanted lots of help, which kept me hopping, but most of the time they went places I'd never been, and I had to let them puzzle it out themselves. Sometimes I was able to refer them to classmate experts.

What methods did you use for evaluating student achievement?

Students kept logs of their work to receive credit for their work. I tracked students' progress daily. Project [proposals] were pre-approved.

"The worst part is that I didn't have time to learn everything that they learned!"

Multiple projects could be open at a time. Students presented me with results in a closing document.

How did the project work out? What feedback did you get from participants?

Students were thrilled. I got thank-you email from parents. A local paper wrote us up. One student, now an enthusiastic computer user, said that she had hardly ever used a computer at home, nor had she wanted to [until becoming involved in this project].

What did the students end up teaching you?

How can I even begin? The worst part is that I didn't have time to learn everything that they learned!

What are your feelings about the effectiveness of the project?

I'm excited when students take their skills beyond what I know. It's a wonderful feeling when you start out with computerphobes and end up with budding experts. The kids are so enthusiastic and spend as much time in the computer lab as they can manage.

What impact do you foresee the Internet having on American students' motivation to learn other languages besides English?

I remember being thrilled when, on a trip to Canada as a preteen, I came home with a cereal box printed in French. I was so isolated that other languages weren't quite real to me, and a prosaic item like that cereal box in a foreign language made a real impression. American kids today aren't that isolated, and the Internet will decrease the isolation even more. It is providing the opportunity and need to use other languages, which will create an even greater desire to learn.

Are there any tips you would like to pass along to other teachers who might want to undertake a similar project?

Let your kids figure out as much by themselves as possible, intervene only when necessary (when you see frustration levels getting too high or can provide tips to make their work more efficient). It is often better to guide and suggest than to try to "teach" how everything is done.

Don't be afraid to try. (Yeah, right, I was scared to death, but I started out with a very friendly class.) We had some problems, but actually things went very smoothly. Just practice some at home first so you are at least a little familiar with the programs. Take your time. You don't have to get fancy right away. I still consider myself a novice. Just open the door and the students will take it from there.

What additional resources would you recommend to these teachers?

Find someone who knows what he/she's doing to help you when you get stuck. This can be a student, community member, a tech ListServ or User Group on the Internet—or all of the above. I rely heavily on EDTECH ListServ at EDTECH@msu.edu; find others through http://www.dejanews.com or your newsgroup provider.

Here is an excerpt of a student log from one of Gary's foreign exchange students from Thailand.

```
1/27 I am back. Today we learned about how to
use all the buttons. It's kind of easy to use
though. We took a note today. Mr. Ankney said
too fast. I wasn't able to catch up, but any-
way, I could see from my friend beside me.
Now, he lets us to play with the screen. I
did it. I'm done now so I will work on the
internet. I might send some mails to my
friends and my family. I'd better get going. I
have only 15 minutes.
```

At the end of the school year, this same student writes of her new-found love of the Internet.

```
5/29 Finally, this day came. I can't believe my year is
almost over. It's beyond believe. I would like to say I
thank you for giving me a chance and opening my eyes to
the new world that I never thought I would like. I do like
computer very much now. I learned so many things from this
class. I'm able to turn on the computer and operate it
other than playing Solitaire. I just don't know what else
to say because there are too much more that I wouldn't be
able to tell you how I feel by writing down in this log.
```

GALLERY

Here is an excerpt of a student log from another one of Gary's foreign exchange students from Russia.

1/23 Today we worked with Operating System MS-DOS. We also studied what to do if the program has a virus, and how to fix it. To check if it has a virus we have to print "cd f-prot, f-prot." Form virus is the easiest virus to destroy. Viruses can copy themselves to another disk every chance they get. They can erase and also change things. I had a virus in my computer and it was very interesting to see what you have to do to destroy the virus.

Now I know that operating environment is a system that makes your system easier to use. I like it very much and I hope that soon I'll be able to use a computer without problems.

Later that week, the same student learns first hand about computer viruses.

1/25 Today I lost all of my notes because of virus. That is why I can not type it today. I am sorry. But I saw a lot of interesting things today. I painted a lot of things. I liked it very much. I am glad that we have a chance to see all this fun things.

FEATURES
The glass pyramid Pei designed to shelter the new underground entrance to the Louvre contained 675 diamond-shaped and 118 triangular panes. The proportions ended up being the same as those of ancient Egyptian pyramids. Pei's team had experimented with other proportions, but eventually concluded that the Egyptians had been correct in defining the ideal proportions.

Are you and your students interested in contacting peers or friends and family in other countries via the Internet? Whether your students come from a small town in Russia or are simply interested in exchanging information with people in other countries, there are many ways for them to correspond internationally with the aid of a computer and online connection.

Share Gary's Story

Discuss Gary's story with your students. Even though Gary didn't set up a specific site, you can discuss the different elements of communication used to relay information back and forth, first via email, and then using audio and visual devices. Discuss the benefits of this mode of exchanging information.

As demonstrated by Gary's students, some benefits of international online communication can be:

- relaying information back-and-forth in real time with minimal cost;
- using foreign language fonts or translation technology to make communication more understandable to people in other countries who may speak minimal English;
- exchanging audio tracks of people's voices, music, or radio broadcasts;
- sharing downloaded images, either still photos or videos.

Research Available Resources

Through much exploration, Gary and his foreign exchange students discovered a host of resources that helped them communicate back home to friends and family using not only written words, but also visual imagery and audio tracks. The first step, of course, was obtaining individual email accounts for students, since a group account proved insufficient. Oftentimes, this can be done without any cost to the school. Check to see who your Internet Service Provider provider is. Like Gary, you may be able to obtain unused teacher accounts, or simply acquire separate accounts for students.

If your students wish to converse in a non-English language that requires different characters, you will need to obtain foreign language fonts. Gary's students discovered where to access some of these through chat rooms, which proved easy to download and install in Windows. Through the search engine Alta Vista, they found a site that explained how to install these fonts for DOS, Windows 3.1, Windows 95 and Macintosh. Shortly thereafter, Gary and his students learned how to use keyboard drivers in the same fashion—by researching, following online directions, and then trying it out.

Gary said that downloading images was quite easy, the key being a decent graphics package. He used Paint Shop Pro and recommended trying Shareware, for which it is very easy to register through schools. The inexpensive full-color scanner which Gary purchased, a MicroTek Scanmaker E3, proved invaluable in relaying photographs to friends and family abroad.

Integrating audio required students to learn to use related programs on their Windows-based platform, but again, Gary admitted that this was surprisingly simple. Some real-time audio, like connecting with radio stations, requires special drivers. Web66 Internet Server Cookbook at http://web66.coled.umn.edu/Cookbook/Default.html provides a step-by-step guide with hypertext links to setting up your system for sound and video.

Establish Goals

The main goal of Gary's project was to help foreign exchange students improve communications with home. Even if you don't have any foreign exchange students, it is likely that ESL or other students might know people abroad with whom they would like to correspond. An alternative would be to set up a "pen pal" or keypal connection online, one through which students could exchange information about their respective countries and cultures using online technology.

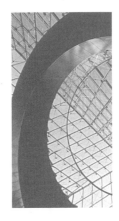

ELEMENTS
When viewed from above, the dramatic spiral of the curved staircase inside the transparent pyramid leads the eye upward. Because of the technical complexity and sensitivity of working in such a historically revered context, the Louvre project was one of the few on which Pei used computer-generated simulations to help envision the impact of the final result.

There are many Web sites that seek to link students from around the world through keypal and multi-lingual chat forums (See Resources, p. 58). KIDLINK at http://www.kidlink.org/ is a not-for-profit Web site that involves students in a variety of international dialogues. When students log on to this site, they choose the language in which they wish to communicate and a dialogue. Five kinds of KIDLINK dialogues exist: Open Email Discussion, Organized Discussions, Special Projects, Real-time Chat, and Art Exchange.

Tracking students' progress is an important aspect of this project, one that can be equally exciting for both teachers and students as they become increasingly proficient online. Gary required students to keep logs of their work in order to receive credit and tracked students' progress daily. Throughout the year, it became apparent that students often set smaller "goals" for themselves, from learning how to use non-English language fonts to figuring out ways to listen to hometown radio stations via computer.

Create Your Own International Exchange

Gary began his class's project by teaching students how to use email. From there, Gary gave students a great deal of freedom to explore possibilities. They visited chat rooms, learned from each other, and received guidance and instruction from Gary when needed. "It is often better to guide and suggest than to try to teach how everything is done," he said.

Learning how to use the appropriate technology before embarking on the project will certainly help students and save some "experimental" time. Having a scanner, a graphics package, and audio-related software will add sophistication to the project; knowledge of foreign language fonts will prove helpful for students who are more comfortable corresponding in a non-English language. Regardless, students who are motivated to communicate and explore the Internet will become quite resourceful, as Gary's story illustrated.

INFLUENCES

"If you have knowledge, let others light their candles at it."

—*Margaret Fuller*

The stories you have read are just a few of the many ways in which non-English languages can be used to learn, communicate, and interact on the Internet. You may want to work with your students to come up with variations on the stories presented, and to discuss the educational benefits of using foreign languages to correspond online.

ONE *Look at the Goals of Your Language Learning or Use*

The teachers featured in this book each began with an objective or goal in mind. Fan wanted to create a medium through which Chinese students could improve their literary skills, gain more confidence in their new American school environment, and maintain ties to fellow Chinese students in the United States and abroad. Sharon's aim was to supplement students' textbook knowledge of Spanish with real-time online interaction in order for them to learn the language from native speakers. Further, she used the Internet as a tool to motivate students to directly apply what they studied, as though they were visiting a Spanish-speaking country. Gary's students differed from the above two in that they were foreign exchange students visiting the states for just a year. Their goal was to figure out ways to effectively communicate back home using online technology, which began for them with the initial aim of learning email and evolved into a sophisticated audiovisual interchange.

Begin by asking students what their goals are or might be for a project of this nature. You may want to start with a discussion of what their personal interests are pertaining to languages and the Internet, since success on the aforementioned projects was in large part due to the students' motivation to learn, explore, and communicate.

Also take into consideration the languages students already speak or are studying when beginning your project. Foreign exchange or ESL students will be more comfortable communicating in their native language, whereas American students who speak only English will likely be using the Internet here to practice a language that's new to them.

Ask your students to think about what level of proficiency is needed to have a meaningful exchange. Defining what is meant by a "meaning-ful exchange" will further clarify this question, and shed light on what students would like to learn from others via the Internet.

Integrate Cultural Studies TWO

A large part of learning a language involves understanding not only grammar and sentence structure, but also the culture on which the language is based. The way people communicate, the words and phrases used, often reflect underlying cultural values and traditions. Under-standing where a person is coming from, their family and community structure, religion, and political environment, are just some of the factors that reflect the way words are communicated.

As Americans, we are very individualistic, whereas many cultures view themselves as part of an extended family structure that is closely enmeshed. We have a great many freedoms that are not present in other cultures—freedom of speech, of choice, of religion, just to name a few. It's easy to make assumptions that other people around the world have the same freedoms and attitudes, but when we communi-cate with others outside the US, we learn that many differences exist.

Learning about other cultures before making the Internet connection will prove helpful in truly understanding the person or people with whom your students will make contact. Fan noted, for example, that his native Asian students couldn't understand why Americans learned to write "love letters" for Valentine's day, since this sort of confession would lead to dating, which meant that the person had all intentions of marrying the other. This small piece of information proved signifi-cant in terms of the way Americans and Asians regard the universal word "love" and the concept of dating. An excellent source of cultural information is the Human Languages Page which is found at http://www.june29.com/HLP/. This site is just one of many that provide resources for or in a particular language, dealing with the language itself and literature in that language (See Resources, p. 62).

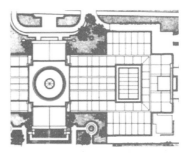

The influence of Frank Lloyd Wright, who pioneered design that emphasized horizontal lines and spaces and innova-tions in the use of concrete and combinations of materials, can be seen in some of Pei's work. Other architects of influence were Mies van der Rohe, Le Corbusier, and Marcel Bruer.

Respecting another's culture indicates respect for that person, which will ensure a more effective dialogue. Discuss with your students the meaning of cultural awareness, and ways they can build understanding of others' cultures. The Internet is a wonderful resource for doing research on cultures around the world. For example, an excellent Internet resource is the Chinese Language Related Information Page at http://www.webcom.com/~bamboo/chinese/chinese.html, which was created by native Chinese speakers to educate others about their language and culture.

Self-awareness is also an important aspect of cultural studies, since it's difficult to recognize differences or similarities with another unless we understand ourselves first. Through words and/or images, ask students to express what comes to mind when they think about their culture. Since Americans come from all over the world, it is likely that their perceptions of other Americans will vary depending on their family's heritage and religion.

THREE *Brainstorm Possible Projects*

Keeping in mind the goals you and your class have decided upon, take some time with your class to brainstorm possible projects. The first area to consider is your access to Internet-related technology:

- What online technology is available to students?
- How much computer experience do students already have?
- How can each student obtain individual email accounts (if applicable)?
- What options are there for acquiring additional support technology?
- How can your school get more hardware/software without incurring significant cost?

Next, decide whether you want to conduct your project as a class group, as independent projects, or as a combination of both:

- Do you want to focus on creating a single class product (like Fan Fang's newsletter) or a more individual-based communications project (as with Gary's class)?
- Do you have enough computers to allow students individual access, or will it require students to work together or in intervals?
- How do the students wish to work?
- How will you best be able to monitor student progress?

One advantage of working as a group is that you can maintain organization and a singular goal towards which all students are working at the same pace. Group projects also offer students the experience of learning how to function as a team. Individual projects, on the other hand, allow students to work independently, which ensures that each student gains hands-on experience. Here, students can work at their own pace and proceed to explore a variety of topics that reflect different areas of interest.

The last step in this process is to review the brainstorming ideas, narrow them down, then work with your class to decide upon and define your project. The more students contribute to shaping this project, the more motivated they will be to participate in it. Here are some questions to consider:

- What are the students most interested in accomplishing through the Internet?
- How will foreign languages be integrated in this project?
- Will the project be sufficiently challenging for all students involved?
- What educational benefits does the project offer?
- How does this project meet your original goals?

If you and your students choose to be part of an existing online project, there are many sites dedicated to international collaborative projects (See Resources, p. 58). For example, Web sites such as I*EARN at http://www.iearn.org/iearn/ encourage students from around the world to telecollaborate via the Internet. Projects range from a group of students investigating various aspects of historical and recent genocide, to a student-written newsletter that discusses environmental issues and describes action plans.

Research Your Project FOUR

Now that you've decided on a project, the next step is to figure out how you will accomplish this task. Researching potential programs, software and hardware in advance will shed light on your options and provide invaluable guidance.

The conceptual source of inspiration Pei began with in designing the East-Wing building of the National Gallery was the Great Library of Alexandria. The new wing was commissioned at a time when American art museums were attracting increasing numbers of visitors, and encouraging the access to great art for the public, not just the elite.

First, take into consideration the technology available to you at the start of your project:

- Does your school have an Internet Service Provider (ISP)?
- How many students can you accommodate at one time?
- What additional technological resources does your school make avaiable to you?
- Do you have a "techie" person on staff who can help you learn more about existing hardware and software?
- What kinds of technology workshops are available for teachers in your district?

Think about the type of technology your project might involve:

- Will you be incorporating graphics, either static or moving?
- If images will be used, what kind of scanning or graphics software do you have?
- Is sound an important factor? If so, what audio-related technology do you have access to?
- Does your project require language translation technology?
- What language fonts might be needed? Keypads?
- Will you need to create a Web site?

The process of researching will likely prove an adventure in itself, providing an array of interesting options for you and your students to explore. The Internet is an ideal research tool, since there are numerous Web sites already established on a wide variety of resource subjects that provide information on where to access various products and also give clear instructions on how to use them.

In addition to Web sites, chat rooms are another mode of online research, since many educators interact and share knowledge this way. Gary's students learned a great deal about language fonts and radio access through chatting with others. Sharon gained further knowledge about MOO technology through real-time online interactions following her training workshop. Yahoo: Chat can be found at http://www.yahoo.com/computers and internet/chat. This site lists chat areas by topic with links to reviews and plug-ins. It is important to note that the content of many IRC chat areas can be rough and uncensored; students connecting to this resource should be carefully supervised (See Resources, p.59).

If you're interested in creating a project similar to Fan's, an effective starting point would be to visit his Web site which is found at http://nisus.sfusd.k12.ca.us/programs/chinese/homepage.htm. Fan has tested a variety of software programs and has provided valuable information here. Although Sharon and Gary's classes did not create Web sites, you might want to refer to the Resources section in the back of this book for listings that might be of interest. It includes a variety of MOO-related foreign language sites, as well as educational resources to help get you started.

An effective offline research method is to simply talk with your fellow teachers. Look on bulletin boards for workshop offerings or related opportunities; read current computer and Web-related magazines to keep you posted on the latest technology. Contacting your school board might also direct you towards potential resources for acquiring additional technology for the school.

Determine Structure for the Project FIVE

Having researched potential ways to approach your class project, you will now be able to determine how you wish to structure it. This book includes different approaches to structuring a class project, ranging from a "learn as you go" method to a more definitive, organized approach.

Fan maintained structure by encouraging students to choose a job on the newsletter in graphic design, editorial, or reporting/writing. He allowed his editorial board to determine the pace of production and establish columns that would appear consistently in the publication.

Sharon maintained organization by giving students handouts to first learn how to use MOO technology, then begin corresponding using the same questions and guidelines for each student. The most consistent element of structure in Gary's class was the requirement for students to keep a daily log. The logs kept Gary in tune with each student's progress and direction throughout the term.

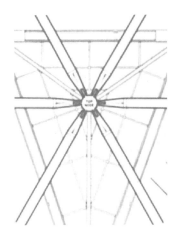

Trips to baroque churches in Germany and Austria inspired Pei in his creation of interior spaces that incorporated light and the movement of people in the National Gallery East-Wing building. Skylights such as the 500-ton welded steel space frame skylight above the courtyard required technological skill and innovation.

Depending on the goals of your project, you can keep the project fairly open and fluid, or maintain a tighter rein in order to complete specific tasks. Consider the following questions:

- How much freedom do you wish students to have as they embark on this project?
- Will they be primarily dependent on you for instruction, or will they simply be guided when issues arise?
- Does the aim of your project require following regimented guidelines, or does it permit students to venture in various directions?

If the goal of your project is to simply learn how to use and interact via online technology, it will naturally lend itself to remaining more flexible and spontaneous, allowing students more creative freedom. However, if your aim is for students to learn or accomplish something very specific and/or time intensive, students will be required to adhere to the guidelines you set in a more structured setting.

SIX Evaluate and Communicate your Project's Effectiveness

Like any other class assignment, you will need to evaluate student work. This can be done in a number of ways, depending on the nature of the project. If students are all following the same template, as with Sharon's project, you can check student work by reading the answers they fill in on their worksheets. Gary's students worked more independently, which did not lend itself to a uniform way of "testing," but rather a more qualitative approach. He had students keep logs of their work in order to track progress. Similarly, Fan's students kept a portfolio of their work.

Among the most effective evaluation methods for Internet-related projects are those that actively involve the student. The more students are directly involved in their project, the more they'll take away from that experience. Active participation rather than passive observation will inevitably lead to greater success for the students. Monitoring student progress and evaluating their work on a regular basis will keep you informed and students motivated.

Sharing information about your class project will provide you and your students with a resource for feedback, teaching others, and communicating with people who are interested in what you are doing. If you are creating a Web site, make sure you list your email address online so others can contact you. Fan noted that Chinese speaking students from all over the world not only participated on newsletter surveys, they also provided helpful feedback. Some even contributed articles.

Other ways to spread the word about your project include sharing information at technology events, computer workshops, or teacher meetings. You can even write up an article and send it to local publications or school technology journals. Gary's project was written up in his town's newspaper, and Fan's was covered in a national magazine on educational technology.

Since online technology projects are still new to most schools, you'll find that fellow educators will likely be very interested in what you are doing. Taking the time to share information and spread the word once your project is underway will surely motivate others to learn more about the Internet's value as an educational tool.

The Pei family's garden retreat in Suzhou, China, was a source of inspiration for Fragrant Hill, a hotel located on the grounds of an ancient imperial hunting estate. Pei superimposed a sketch of his hotel design onto a traditional Chinese drawing to convince the Chinese of its suitability for the setting.

Keypals

SchoolWorld Keypal Project
http://www.schoolworld.asn.au/keypals.html
Rendez-vous is a free penfriend and keypal service. Students can select a penpal/keypal from more than 20 languages, select a level of fluency or choose a language and level for themselves.

International E-Mail Tandem Network
http://marvin.uni-trier.de/Tandem/email/infen.html
This project is made up of a number of bilingual subnets, in which learners of different native languages work together in order to help each other learn, through mailing lists and individual email.

Intercultural E-Mail Classroom Connections
http://www.stolaf.edu/network/iecc/
The IECC mailing lists are a free service to help teachers and classes link with partners in other countries and cultures.

Collaborative Projects

Telecollaborating Around the World
http://www1.minn.net/~schubert/NickNacks.html
This site encourages telecollaboration among educators and students around the world.

International Schools Cyberfair
http://www.gsn.org/gsn/cb
Students from K-12 are invited to participate in this international fair by creating World Wide Web sites that highlight what's special about their own community. Email cyberfair-helper@gsn.org or call 619-721-2972 for more information.

Language Learning Activities for the World Wide Web
http://polyglot.lss.wisc.edu/lss/lang/nflrc.html
A place to get ideas for a collaborative, bilingual Internet project.

RESOURCES

Chat

InterLinks: IRC
http://alabanza.com/kabacoff/Inter-Links/irc.html
An overview of IRC with links to tools that will help you
begin "chatting."

Yahoo: Chat
http://www.yahoo.com/Computers and Internet/chat
Chat sites are listed by topic with links to reviews and plug-ins.

The Language Academy
http://sf.bilingual.net.
A collection of chat rooms and bulletin boards related to ESL and
bilingual education with links to national bilingual organizations.

Keypals Club International Chat
http://worldkids.net/welcome.htm
World Kids Net has several ways for kids from all around the world
to keep in touch.

MOOs & MUDs

MOO Teacher's Tip Sheet
http://www.daedalus.com/net/MOOTIPS.html
A good overview of MOOs and how to use them in the classroom.
Includes a step-by-step introduction to using a MOO that can be
downloaded as a handout for students.

MUDs, MOOs, MUSHs
http://www.itp.berkeley.edu/~thorne/MOO.html
Provides an extensive list with links of educational foreign language
and EFL/ESL Multi-user Domains (MUD), Object Oriented MUD (MOO)
and Multi-user Shared Hallucination (MUSH).

schMOOze University
http://schmooze.hunter.cuny.edu:8888/
telnet schmooze.hunter.cuny.edu 8888
Students have opportunities to practice English in one-on-one and
group conversations as well as access to language games, an on-line
dictionary, USENET feed, and gopher access.

For the world-class symphony center Pei designed for the city of Dallas, Pei sought to evoke the grandeur of the Paris Opera and stylistic elements of Baroque music halls in Europe.

MundoHispano
http://web.syr.edu/~lmturbee/mundo.html
telnet europa.syr.edu 8888
This web site is a great place to introduce students to the variety of
activities available in a foreign language MOO.

Cafe MOOlano
telnet moolano.berkeley.edu 8888.
A multi-language educational MOO.

Diversity University
telnet moo.du.org 8888
A multi-language educational MOO

ArdaMOO,
telnet lince.las.es 7777
A Spanish language social MOO.

Le MOO Francais,
telnet moo.syr.edu 7777
A French langauge MOO.

"LittleItaly",
telnet little.usr.dsi.unimi.it 4444
An Italian MOO.

MorgenGrauen LPmud,
telnet mud.uni-muenster.de 23
A German language MUD.

UNItopia,
telnet infosgi.rus.uni-stuttgart.de:3333
A German language MUD.

MOOsaico,
telnet moo.di.uminho.pt 7777
A Portuguese language MOO.

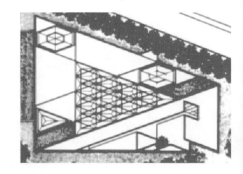

SvenskMud,
telnet svmud.lysator.liu.se 2043
A Swedish language MUD .

Newsgroups

USENET Info Center Launch Pad
http://sunsite.oit.unc.edu/usenet-i/home.html
This beginner's guide to Internet newsgroups is a by-subject guide
to usenet groups.

Deja News
http://www.dejanews.com
An easy-to-use searchable database for online newsgroups.

EDTECH
The EDTECH ListServ provides technical help and can be accessed
by emailing EDTECH@mus.edu.

Language-related Newsgroups
The following newsgroups offer bilingual practice with
native speakers:
k12.lang.deutsch-eng (German/English)
k12.lang.esp-eng (Spanish/English)
k12.lang.francais (French)
k12.lang.japanese (Japanese/English)
k12.lang.russian (Russian/English)

Teacher Resources

Foreign Language Resources on the Web
http://www.itp.berkeley.edu/~thorne/HumanResources.html
Provides links to the best of the foreign language Web sites available.

The Yamada Language Center
http://babel.uoregon.edu/Yamada.html
The definitive archive of non-English fonts and language-related Web
connections and newsgroups.

Language Index
http://www.sussex.ac.uk/langc/langs.html
This powerful site offers links to the resources and software you need to
communicate online in the following languages: Chinese, French,
German, Italian, Japanese, Russian and Spanish.

The idea of using a pyramid for the Louvre entrance came from Pei's studies of the works of Le Notre, a French landscape architect, whose plantings were arranged geometrically. The pyramid when viewed from above is a square, a shape in which Le Notre often arranged plantings.

Foreign Language for Travelers
http://www.travlang.com
Free lessons in over 50 different languages. Audio clips recorded by native speakers and Quizzes help students to learn each language.

Foreign Language Learning Resources
http://www.call.gov/
A good source for foreign language newspapers and teacher resources for less commonly taught languages.

Classroom Connect Resources

Classroom Connect Web Site
http://www.classroom.com
Great resources for teachers.